THE POWER TO OBTAIN OPTIMUM HEALTH & NUTRITION

BY BISHOP DENNIS LEONARD

THE POWER TO OBTAIN OPTIMUM HEALTH & NUTRITION

BY BISHOP DENNIS LEONARD

Published in Denver, Colorado,
by Dennis Leonard Publishing
www.dennisleonardministries.com
ISBN   1-880809-16-8

Printed In The United States of America

Contents

DEDICATION

I would like to give special thanks to my outstanding wife, Michele, for her insight and wisdom on the subject of health and nutrition. I would like to thank her for the time that she dedicated into the preparation of this book.

I would also like to thank all of those who have submitted their testimonies to me via the mail and my website, www.dennisleonardministries.com...and encouraged me to compile this topic into written form.

Remember, your best days are still ahead!

Bishop Dennis Leonard

INTRODUCTION

"Know ye not that ye are the temple of God, and that the Spirit of God dwelleth in you? If any man defile the temple of God, him shall God destroy; for the temple of God is holy, which temple ye are. Let no man deceive himself. If any man among you seemeth to be wise in this world, let him become a fool, that he may be wise."
I Corinthians 3:16-18

Friend, it is time to get our health in order…The Bible way. As our creator, God knows what works best for us mentally and physically. We have tried every kind of medical and or diet program but have only seen temporary results. It is time to go back to the Bible. The Bible tells us that in the beginning God created the heavens and the earth (Genesis 1:1). We were created from the dust of the earth and from natural elements. The majority of our bodies are also made up of minerals and water. In fact, 70% of your body is water.

God made our bodies perfect. He made us in such a way that if our bodies are nourished properly, they will never get sick. It's all very simple, obey all of God's Word and all that is in it and be blessed. This world itself is cursed because of man falling into sin but Jesus came to redeem us from the curse (Ephesians 1:7 paraphrased).

If you are going through a difficult situation today, I want to encourage you to log onto my website at www.dennisleonardministries.com...there are countless numbers of materials there to help you today. You can also email your prayer requests or even your testimonies. God has a great plan for you!

Your best days are still ahead,

Bishop Dennis Leonard

1

THE POWER TO OBTAIN
OPTIMUM HEALTH & NUTRITION

"And God said, Behold, I have given you every herb bearing seed, which is upon the face of all the earth, and every tree, in the which is the fruit of a tree yielding seed; to you it shall be for meat."
Genesis 1:29

If you will look in the Bible, you can see what God intended for our diets to look like. From the beginning, He intended for us to eat seeds, nuts, fruits and vegetables. We were to drink lots of water which would help to flush our system. But we human beings have messed everything up. Today's diets include lots of meat that's filled with hormones and toxins. We frequently consume sugar, which shuts down our immune systems. We love white flour, which turns to paste in our bodies. If you don't believe it, think back to when you were in grade school and you made paste using white flour and water! There is no nutrition of any value in white flour.

The bottom line is that we are not obeying the Word of God, and we are sick, over weight and unhealthy. We are killing ourselves with our diet, and are missing God's best for our lives. A while back, I became burdened for the body of Christ in this area. I see so many people being buried in their forties, fifties and sixties when God intended for us to live a minimum of seventy or more years. To live in optimum health, you must eat for nutrition and health, build a strong immune system, exercise and get plenty of rest. Sound easy? It really is if you determine in your mind that you are committed to a lifestyle of health.

As a child of God, you must know that your body is the temple of the Holy Spirit. How can you continually put things in your body that is killing you? "But Bishop, it tastes so good." I know the food may taste good but do you really know what it is doing to you? Hosea (4:6) tells us, "My people are destroyed for lack of knowledge…" It is time to gain the knowledge you need in every area of your life. You are not just a spirit but you are body, soul and spirit. You have to minister to all three areas of your life. You go to church, read your Bible and pray for the spiritual part. But for the most part, Christians do not take care of their bodies they way they should. When you are a believer in God's Word, you must make up your mind to quit doing things the world's way and do them God's way. If you will come into agreement with God's Word today, it could save your life. This book is about saving lives for the Kingdom of God.

2

TAKE CARE OF YOURSELF

God made our bodies so perfect, that if you give it proper nutrition, it can take great care of itself. If you get a small cut on your finger, all you have to do is wait a few days and that cut will heal itself. God made you in such a way that if you will obey His Word, He will put none of the sicknesses on you that He put on the sinner (Exodus 15:26 paraphrased). Tell yourself right now, "I don't have to be sick." Hallelujah!

God says, "And all these blessings shall come on thee, and overtake thee, if thou shalt hearken unto the voice of the Lord thy God" (Deuteronomy 28:2 paraphrased). You start by repenting of your sins in order to receive forgiveness.

Sometimes you have to stop and repent of the stuff you have done to your own body. How many times have you "stuffed" yourself at the local buffet? Or maybe you just eat junk foods and sweets all day long. The damage this does to your body can take many different forms. But from the beginning, God designed raw foods to bring nutrition and healing to the human body. He wants to heal us of all our diseases and sicknesses. But we must repent of doing things the world's way and not His way.

We are all afraid of germs, viruses and bacteria. But you need to know that if you are healthy and have a strong immune system, your body can overcome anything. If you get sick, it's because of a weak immune system. God made you capable of fighting off those things, which would come against you. So the key to living a healthy life is to build up your immune system.

I know that some of this information is not easy for you to accept. Did you know that there is strong evidence that certain meats, dairy products, sugar, salt, white flour and processed foods are robbing people of a healthy and long life? Remember that a "snack" is supposed to replenish your body and energy. But most people just please their taste buds not realizing they are putting nutritional stress on their bodies. So, stop and tell yourself right now, "I don't have to be sick." The body has over 100 trillion cells in it. But it replaces every cell within one year.

That is amazing. If you started making changes today, you could get your entire body renewed within 12 months. How exciting is that? It is like a fresh start to health!

"Well Preacher, this sounds good but I don't know if I can do it." If you will listen to the Word of God today and make some changes, you can see results that will change your future and your destiny. Are you willing to obey God's Word in order to feel better and to live a long life? You need to know that God's Word is always true. If you put junk in your body, then you cannot live a healthy and energetic life. If you're always tired and sick, you need to make some changes today. God's Word says that it's His will that we prosper and be in health as our soul prospers (3 John 2). God is bringing you some information today that will allow you to fulfill your purpose and your destiny in this life. It is really this simple: Obey the Word of God and live; Disobey the Word of God and die!

We cannot continually eat processed foods that are filled with chemicals and expect God to heal us over and over again. You must put down foods that are high in fat and sugar if you expect to live a healthy life. You don't have to be overweight and unhealthy to die of a heart attack at 47 years old. My wife, Michele, and I really made a commitment to cutting things out of our diet and making some changes. But let me be clear, we do not diet. I am the first to admit that I cannot stay on a diet.

My wife can, but I can't. When I say diet, I mean our way of eating. The choices we make. We simply began to change the foods that we ate and within two weeks we had lost five pounds each. We ate as much as we wanted to eat but simply changed the things that we ate. Hard to believe? Well, it is absolutely true. When you eat the right things, you can eat a lot more and still lose weight and be healthy.

Well, you may be saying, "I don't need to lose weight." This is not about losing weight although it can help you achieve that goal also. This is about eating right so that you can fulfill your Godly purpose and destiny. Listen to this. You don't have to have high blood pressure and die from a heart attack. Even if every member of your family died at a young age from a heart attack, you don't have to have the same outcome. Maybe sugar diabetes runs in your family. Break that curse right now! You don't have to struggle with adult diabetes and continually be sick. But you have to start using your faith, pray in a different way and change your diet.

Your body was not designed to process foods that were saturated with preservatives, chemicals and hormones. If you look at the product label, they will list words you cannot even pronounce. That is a signal to slowly put the package down and run for your life. Your system was not created to continually consume foods that are unnatural and filled with sugar and have high contents of fat. The truth is that the American diet is causing us to be the heaviest and most overweight people on the earth. Our food tastes soooo good, but it's killing us. We know how to take the worst of foods and make them taste wonderful. They are saturated in fat and soaked in sugar. It's time to tell the truth and shame the devil. I want you to live a long and healthy life.

God has a great plan for you, but if you allow obesity or an unhealthy diet dictate your destiny because you are strapped with being tired all the time or you're always sick, you'll miss what God has for you. If you are struggling with your weight or you are sick in your body, I want you to email your prayer request to me today at www.dennisleonardministries.com. I want to pray and come in agreement with you over your needs.

3

"My Momma was Sick, Grandma was Sick...well..."

"Bishop, my whole family has these same health problems." We all know that generational curses run in families. But if you'll look at the diets within a family, you'll usually see why heart disease and sugar diabetes is generational. The health problems are probably the result of long time horrible eating habits. The answer to this family problem can start with healing but there will also have to be some diet changes or this problem will return. If your eating is out of control; you will not overcome that illness. What you really have to do is crucify your flesh. Oh, I know I am all up in your business now; but it's because I love you and want the best for you.

My own father had a heart attack in his sixties and almost

died. He had to have triple by-pass heart surgery. The mercy of God kept him alive. His diet consisted of fried foods, saturated fats and even though he worked hard, he did not exercise on a regular basis. God spoke to my heart some years ago and said, "If you don't change, the same things that happened to your dad will happen to you." Friend, you can say, "In the name of Jesus, I break that generational curse." But if you don't change your diet, your prayer will not accomplish a whole lot. You are actually fighting against the very prayer that you are praying when you eat the wrong things. Your life is not in agreement with your prayer.

"But Bishop, I went to the doctor and he put me on medication." All of us know people who take pills for high blood pressure. Others take pills to thin their blood. The goal is to take all of these drugs in order to be healed. But the truth of the matter is that drugs only treat a symptom. Drugs do not heal. Medication is great. I thank God for all the breakthroughs in medicine to help people. But we need God's wisdom and help in preventing the illness to begin with. The Bible says that God's ways are higher than man's ways (Isaiah 55:9 paraphrased). That's why we must go to God's Word and do what God says. Yes, I believe in healing, but isn't health better than healing? Say it now, "I need to change."

As a pastor, it bothers me to see God's people sick and

dying too early. I hate going to a funeral of somebody that died too early because they would not change their diet. It saddens me to see God's people going from doctor to doctor, and not getting any better. They spend hundreds or thousands of dollars on medication and they don't get any better. Last year, American people spent over 110 billion dollars on medicine! Many times people go to the doctor and he says, "I know you are sick and you have these symptoms but I can't find out what is wrong with you." Doctors are great...but they did not create you. God did and He can best tell you how to get well and stay well.

I am convinced that good nutrition along with faith and prayer can heal almost anything that's wrong in your body. I've seen people change their diets and within weeks were able to cut way back on medication. I am not telling you to cut out doctors, I believe in doctors. I thank God for doctors. When you make some big changes in your life and diet, you need to check with your doctor. I want to give you an example of what I am talking about. I know people who have had diabetes from a child (Type 1 diabetes) and had to take shots every day. When they changed their diet, they were able to cut way back on the insulin almost immediately. I have also seen adults who had Type 2 diabetes and changed their diets and saw immediate results in their health. This was done under the supervision of their own physician of course.

"Bishop, what about faith for total healing?" I am not saying we don't need faith in God. We need faith in God. I have seen miraculous healings of every kind. But what I am also telling you is God has provided a way to health for us through our eating. It was not His intention that we would spend half of our lives sick and unable to function. Heart disease is the number one killer of all Americans. Fifty percent of all deaths in America are a result of heart attacks and strokes. God tells us that we don't have to die this way. We know that 1 million Americans die from heart disease every year, and a half million die from cancer. One out of three Americans will develop cancer at some point in their lifetime. Something needs to change. Nutritionists and dietitians tell us that most illness can be corrected with diet.

Saints, this is a wake-up call. We are facing disease at an alarming rate. Cancer is killing more children today than any other disease. Imagine that. Could it be the sugar and the fat in their diets? We know that our children are entering puberty at an earlier age today. I read that the reason is because of the hormones that are put in meat. People think that to eat healthy costs a lot of money. You would be surprised how much lower your grocery bill would be if you cut out the majority of meat, sugar and processed foods. My wife and I began to read up on good nutrition, health and how to live longer. We went to the grocery and loaded up the cart to the top, overflowing. I had a 25 pound bag of carrots underneath the cart, in addition to all that was in the top part. The grocery bill was half of what is normally is. What I am telling you is that the majority of the cost that you are spending is meat, sugar and processed food. Fruits and vegetables are a bargain compared to what those items cost.

4

So, What Does Healthy Eating Look Like, Pastor?

So what should your diet look like today? Always think in terms of dead food verses live or raw food. Fruits and vegetables are live, while processed foods and meat are dead. No matter what it is, if it is processed, it is dead. It might fill your stomach but it won't help you to feel better and walk in health. Processed foods taste good because they are loaded with sugar and salt and fat. Think in terms of live food versus dead food when you select your meals. For example: if a food is cooked it is considered dead. Cooking takes out the vitamins and minerals that would give life to your body. Do feel tired all day long even after you eat? Your food is not energizing you as it should!

Packaged macaroni and cheese tastes good but does not

give life to your body. Salad greens are live food. Corn on the cob would not necessarily be a live food, because it is cooked. It is not all bad because it has fiber and nutrients, but it does lose something in the cooking process. Coleslaw is a live food. It stands to reason that if the human body is made up of water and minerals then it will require living and natural foods in order to sustain good health. If you adhere to this word, it can save you or a family member from a life of illness and possibly death. Isn't it worth that? Aren't you tired of seeing your family members suffer from ill health. You cannot have a high quality of life when you can't get around and don't even feel like doing anything.

One lady told me, "Bishop stay out of my food and leave my meat alone." I'm not saying that you can't have meat. But you shouldn't eat red meat over two or three times per month. Okay, pick yourself up off the floor. It is best for your body if you only eat red meat two or three times per month. Anyway, you don't need near as much meat as you think. Your mind tells you that you need meat to be strong, but don't forget that the gorilla and the elephant don't eat meat. I knew of a body builder who had a contest and proved that he was stronger eating just fruits and vegetables than many others who ate meat on a regular basis.

"Preacher, just tell me why is meat so bad?" One of the reasons meat is not as healthy as it could be is because of how it is raised. Animals are fed with ingredients to make them bigger faster so that they can be sold. Also, many of the illnesses we have today are a result of the fat in animal products. This fat holds no nutritional value but many people love the taste it brings to food. When you remove the fat, your body can function much more efficiently. Maybe you should start by cutting back a little on the meat you are eating and buy leaner cuts. Snack foods are a regular staple to most people. We eat them for breaks, with meals and in the evenings. Included are all kinds of chips—potato chips, corn chips, etc. They are fried until they are crisp and seasoned with wonderful taste delights. But all that oil is bad, bad, bad for your system. Instead of all that hydrogenated oil which is in fried foods, try some baked chips. They might not taste quite as good but it is better for you.

"Bishop, I am not sick. I feel fine so why should I care about my diet." If you are healthy and are never sick you may not understand what I am talking about. But if you are at a point in your life where you have to have more energy and strength, then you probably need to change your diet. If you are not, just wait a few years and you will start to understand. Then get ready and make some changes in your life.

Here is another word on miraculous healing based on diet. I have read about people who have had tumors and when they cut the fat out of their diet, the tumors shriveled and dried up.

Did you know that cancers are simply runaway cells that multiply out of control? Tumors are pockets of toxins and maverick cells that your body is trying to dispose of. When your immune system is operating properly, it gobbles up these maverick cells and spits them out. Every one of us has those bad cells in our bodies. The question is will your immune system be able to fight them off when they gather together. Statistically, one out of eight women will develop breast cancer. The major reason is that women ingest toxins through the meat and food they eat. These toxins are stored in the fattest portion of their bodies, which is the breast. So doesn't it stand to reason that if you are careful about the fats you put into your body and drink lots of water that you will lower your risk of breast cancer.

Most Americans are already in the process of developing cancer due to a lack of exercise, high stress and consumption of processed foods, sugar and fats. But if we'll make some changes today…God will begin the healing process. It doesn't matter how badly you have treated your body. In one year, if you will be careful to do all that is in the manufacturer's book (the Bible), you will see your body completely renewed. Forty-nine percent of all Americans will develop some form of cancer. But only fourteen percent who exercise regularly will develop cancer. That's because exercise helps to work the toxins out of your system. It does not mean you have to go and buy expensive exercise equipment. All you have to do is get on a routine of walking briskly for about twenty minutes, four days a week. Or, get a bike and ride several times a week. It is time to get busy improving your health.

5

You mean, I have to Exercise too?

Another person who is in danger for disease is the person who is very active and does not see a need for exercise. Active people oftentimes think they are healthy. But there can still be plaque building up in your arteries. Unless your heart is pumping at a certain rate for twenty straight minutes; you are at risk for artery blockage. Exercise is very important for a healthy life for everybody. In order for the cells to function properly, body fluids must be kept moving. Exercise puts oxygen in the blood, which maintains good health. When exercise is neglected, all the cells in the body become weakened. But exercise helps eliminate the waste and toxins out of the cells.

"Bishop, my grandma ate pork, beef and all kinds of bad

things her whole life." Our grandparents could eat all the hogfat they wanted and live to be one hundred years old. Why? Because after they ate their eggs and bacon, they went to the field or factory and worked every bit of it out of their system. Now, you eat whatever you will and then go sit in front of the television or the computer. I know this may sound rough to you, but I am concerned about saving somebody's life. The Bible says, "…Whatever a man sows, that shall he also reap" (Galatians 6:7 paraphrased)." I don't care how many times you come up front for prayer, if you don't obey God's laws of nature, you will destroy yourself.

What we want is for all of our food to taste great and be the way we want it to be. But God has already told us to live a disciplined life and crucify our flesh. If you are waiting for God to take away your desire for ice cream or fried chicken—it's not going to happen. You can still bake your chicken and pull the fat off. God says, "I have set before you life and death, blessing and cursing, therefore choose life so that you and your children may live" (Deuteronomy 30:19 paraphrased). It's time to make some choices that will turn your life and your children's lives around. Remember, an ounce of prevention is better than a pound of cure.

I've seen so many people come up front for prayer. They have this thing wrong with them, and that thing. Most of the time, all they'd have to do is lose a 100 pounds and everything would be alright. Let me give you a simple rule to help you build up your immune system and live a healthy life. Try and make 75 percent of your food intake raw. Man is the only creature on this earth that destroys his food by cooking it before he eats it. It's time to rearrange our thinking if you are going to eat right.

If you cook a little bit of cabbage and broccoli and put it with your meal, you get very few vitamins and minerals out of it. You cannot get enough out of it to really live a healthy life. I highly recommend juicing to get the most nutrition out of your vegetables. A juicer removes the pure liquid from the vegetables giving you pure vitamins and minerals. Therefore, use a juicer to drink your vegetables and eat your fruit.

Here is one of my favorite juice recipes. Everyday I juice six carrots, a handful of fresh parsley, a stalk of celery and a forth of an apple. Sometimes I put in a handful of spinach leaves, which are very good for you. Mix it well. This helps to clean out my liver and insides. You can alternate with broccoli and other vegetables that you have on hand. Every so often I will put a beet in because they are so good for you. You see, the nutrition is in the juice. It may not look good to you—but, man, is it good for you. You can do this every morning before you go to work and in the evening after you come home. Are you starting to see how much nutrition you are putting into your body? When I drink this…within one minute I can feel the nutrition going through my body. There is no process time. A juicer is a small investment for such tremendous results.

For breakfast, I often take strawberries and mix them with vanilla lowfat yogurt—they are great together. An example of a lunch I might have is this. It begins with shredded cabbage, grated celery and raisins, walnuts and one half of an apple. It is delicious just like that with no dressing on it. I eat a huge bowl of this and don't have to worry about gaining any weight. You probably already know, dieting does not work. It is also important to drink as much distilled water as possible while cutting back on all meat and dairy products. Eliminate all hydrogenated oils, including all margarine and vegetable oils. That means no peanut butter. If you want to build up your immune system, you have to eliminate all white sugar. Thirty teaspoons of sugar will shut down your immune system for 24 hours. One can of soda contains ten teaspoons! Many, many foods have "hidden sugar" in them. Become a discriminate label reader. I know you are craving sugar, but do you know why? The reason you crave sugar is because it's actually a drug and you are addicted. It is time to break that no good addiction now.

Okay, I am not without sympathy. I kind of like sweets

myself. When we were born, we had a taste for sweets. So let me help you. This may surprise you but nuts help to curb a sweet tooth. Several kinds of nuts are actually good for you, almonds and walnuts for example. Now there is fat in almonds but it is the right kind of fat. Another good nut is pumpkinseeds. Peanuts and pecans have the wrong kind of fat. But here is what I do when I have a taste for sweets, I take a handful of almonds and walnuts and mix with dried apricots and raw honey. It tastes wonderful and completely takes away the desire for sugar.

Be aware, the ways of this world can lead to destruction. If you are not careful—simple, ordinary food will destroy you and cause you to die early and miss your destiny. Here are some other things you can do for sugar substitutes. You can make a pie crust out of grape nuts cereal and frozen apple concentrate. Or use raw almonds and pitted dates. You can use Stevia as a sugar substitute that is all natural for tea or drinks. Also, make sure that you have the right kind of fruit in your house, in your car and at your office. Eat all you want. That would be the juicy type of fruits, pears, plums, apples, peaches, grapes, oranges, etc.

What we are doing is trying to eat right to nourish the body and boost our immune systems. Did you know that caffeine can suppress the immune system by upsetting ones mineral balance? In other words, caffeine keeps your body from absorbing essential minerals. What I have done is cut back on how much coffee I use. Table salt will also shut down your immune system. That's why you should use sea salt or salt substitutes. We use a lot of lime and lemon juice to add flavor instead of salt.

In general, people eat lots and lots of bread with their diets. Make sure you replace white bread with whole grain breads. In white bread, all of the nutrients are removed and then it is bleached to make it white. You might as well eat cardboard. We are told to drink milk for strong bones and teeth. But we are not told that pasteurizing heats all the nutrients out of the milk. Try soymilk with vanilla. When cooking, don't use the fat of animals. Use extra virgin olive oil or raw flaxseed oil. The fat that's in olive oil is actually very good for you. But keep in mind, the more you cook your food, the worse it is.

If you'll make some changes today, you will see some results take place immediately. If you'll start drinking vegetable juice and eating properly, you'll feel great changes in your body. For a long time, we selected juice as a healthy nutritional choice. But if you're going to put proper nutrition in your body, avoid all canned juices. They are very high in sugar. Also, instead of ice cream, eat low sugar and low fat frozen yogurt. "But Bishop, this is going to be tough." It's okay to blow it once in a while…but start to make changes for the good of your own future.

Make it a point to eat foods that are high in fiber. Fiber pushes food through your system and is necessary to maintain good health. Replace white rice with brown rice. Brown rice holds much, much more nutrients than white rice. Broil your meats instead of frying them. "Bishop, I am hungry all the time." The reason you're hungry all the time is because you keep putting junk in your body, and your body is craving nutrition. But when you put good nutrition in your body, the cravings go away. Almost all sickness and disease can be corrected by changing ones nutrition and lifestyle. We feed our young people chips and sugar, and wonder why they're overweight. Slowly make the changes to bring health to your family through good nutrition.

The doctor's say that they don't know the cause of arthritis and many other diseases. But when proper nutrition is in place, conditions improve and many times "mysterious" pains goes away. In fact, when someone is in good physical health it usually causes them to be in good mental health. When you're healthy physically, depression seems to go away. One year from now almost every cell in your body can be replaced. Therefore, one year from now you can have a new body. Are you ready for a new body?

Where will you be one year from now? Your body will be stronger or weaker than it is now. You are either building your body up or you are tearing it down. It's up to you. This generation is sick and getting sicker. If you will obey God's Word, you can live under the blessing instead of the curse. The choice is yours today. When you first start this new way of eating, your body will go through an adjustment. But after a few weeks, you will work the toxins out of your body and you will feel wonderful. Give God's way a chance and realize a healthier, stronger you!

FULFILL YOUR DESTINY

"Know ye not that ye are the temple of God, and that the Spirit of God dwelleth in you?"
I Corinthians 3:16

God desires for you to prosper and be in health (3 John 2). Many people separate their health from their spirit man. They know that God is concerned about their spiritual growth, but don't think He is very interested in their health. But you are body, soul and spirit. If you only take care of your spirit man, you will be out of balance. If you just take care of your physical body and not your spirit, you are still out of balance. If you don't take care of your physical self—you can become weak and die.

When you are healthy and strong physically, you are stronger spiritually. When you are sick; you can hardly hear from God. If you don't feel well, you don't want to go to church or read your Bible. You just want to lie there until the illness is gone. It is hard to function well, when you are "under the weather." If your body is healthy and strong, you will do more for God than if your body is weak and tired. If you are physically tired much of the time, I am suggesting to you that you examine your health, nutrition and understand that it all ties together.

"Bishop, is God really that interested in my health? I feel pretty good." Yes, God wants you to be in the best health possible. Because your body is the temple of the Holy Spirit, you now have an obligation to take care of it. Just the same as you take care of your spirit man, be in church, pay your tithes and study the Word. I love you enough to tell you what you need to hear. If you continue to eat those high fat, fried foods and sugar laden sweets, your body will eventually break down.

Have you ever eaten a meal and immediately felt awful? Some of the foods we consume are just not good for us. They don't fuel the body and they actually cause problems. Heart disease, diabetes, and clogged arteries—they don't just come from nowhere. There is always a cause and the root of the cause is in your food. And let me also say, it doesn't matter if you are very skinny or over weight, you can be dying of heart disease or suffering from diabetes.

In our country today, almost half of all Americans die from heart attacks and strokes. If it is not a heart attack or a stroke, it is cancer. Don't be a statistic! Only fourteen percent of people who exercise get cancer. You can take positive steps through good nutrition and exercise that will help you overcome any health problem. The kind of exercise that I am talking about is working strenuously with your heart pumping for about twenty minutes straight. Find an activity you enjoy and incorporate it into your life. I know you believe in prayer; but prayer alone is not enough. "Bishop, what do you mean, prayer is not enough?" Don't misunderstand me. I totally believe in the healing power of Jesus. What I am saying is that if you are healed and still go back to the same way of life…you will end up having the same problems. Don't be so spiritual that you miss God. Sometimes the things called "generational curses" are brought on by the things you are doing and can be overcome. It's time to wise up and enjoy the destiny God has given you to the fulfill.

Wouldn't it be a shame to come to the end of your life and discover that you died early, and you did not fulfill your destiny because of improper nutrition? Food is like a religion to most Christians. Christians don't drink, don't smoke, don't chew but they sure can eat. Food can be a holy cow if you don't watch out. "Bishop, stay away from my supper table." I am going to help you take the things off of your supper table that are killing you! Listen to this; five thousand people will die of heart disease this year even though it is one of the most treatable afflictions around. All you have to do is make some simple diet changes today and you can live a long life. Remember that every cell in your body replaces itself every twelve months. If you use proper nutrition and exercise, in one year you won't know yourself. Aren't you ready to go for it?

The Bible says that life is in the blood. It's the blood that delivers the necessary oxygen and nutrients to all the cells in your body. It's the blood that removes cellular debris and waste. That's why it's so important to take care of the heart. Every day the heart pumps 5,000 gallons of blood through arteries, veins and blood vessels. If any of these passageways gets clogged, it can be devastating. The body is an incredible machine. God made us in such a way that if you feed it proper nutrition, it would heal itself. You can avoid a trip to the operating room if you will make some changes today.

Your body is constantly repairing itself. When your arteries need repairing, your body pulls nutrients out of the blood system and repairs them. If there are not proper nutrients in your blood, your body uses the cholesterol instead. This is not a good thing. Anytime cholesterol builds up in your arteries, it can cause a heart attack or stroke. But if you will reduce the amount of animal fat in your diet, you can reduce your risk of heart problems. Make sure your body receives the nutrients it needs to function every day. Even if you have heart disease today, there is a lot you can do to turn it around. Clogged arteries can even be reversed without surgery, if you will consult your doctor, exercise and take in proper nutrition.

I want you to be healthy and whole. I want you to fulfill your destiny. Perhaps you need a word of encouragement and there's nobody around to encourage you? If you will log onto my website, www.dennisleonardministries.com...each day there is a Daily Devotion that will help and encourage you. Leave it on your desktop or print it out. Refer to it and read it several times a day. If you have never done this before, you will be surprised and amazed at how much the Word will lift you and encourage you. The joy of the Lord is your strength today!

7

UNDERSTANDING
HOW FOOD AFFECTS YOUR BODY

When we eat food, the body burns it for energy. But this process leaves dangerous by products in the blood known as "free radicals." These free radicals can be very dangerous. When left alone, they can cluster and cause tumors and cancerous growths. Antioxidants are God's way of fighting the free radicals. Antioxidants are amazing substances that actually repair damage from free radicals. Vitamin B, Vitamin C and Vitamin E are great antioxidants. When they are present, they gather around the free radicals and literally gobble them up. These vitamins are mainly available through fruit and fresh vegetables.

If you have an inadequate supply of antioxidants in your diet, then your body is building up plaque in all its arteries and blood vessels. Hosea 4:6 says, "My people are destroyed for lack of knowledge…" It's time to get some knowledge and gain some health. If you take multivitamins, that is good. But you may have to add more of certain vitamins to get what you need. I personally take extra E, C and B. If you don't eat right and you take vitamin supplements you are wasting your money. The majority of your antioxidants have to come through proper nutrition. The vitamins attach themselves to the food in your stomach.

Remember, we are talking about a lifestyle of eating live food versus dead food. If you are going to be healthy, you must put live food in your body. The more you cook food, the more you cook the vitamins and minerals out of it. That's why you should eat your vegetables raw. But if you do cook them, you should steam them rather than boiling them. Have you noticed the color of the water after you boil some vegetables? For example corn, when it is finished cooking, the water is yellow. The reason being is that you cooked all of the vitamins and minerals out of it and it went into the water. If you cook broccoli, the water is green. Once again you cooked out all of the vitamins and minerals.

Maybe you think you need to eat meat with every meal, but you don't. A meal of all vegetables is great and easy to digest. If you are concerned about getting enough protein, try nuts, fish, low-fat cheese, tofu, eggs, turkey and chicken. Even some vegetables have protein and are much better for you.

I have to say something about smoking and your heart. The reason that smoking is so bad for the heart is because the lining of the coronary arteries is comprised of very sensitive cells. They are very easily damaged by free radicals that come from smoking. Smoking is absolutely one of the worst things you could do to your body. In addition to what it does to your lungs, it destroys the arteries to your heart. Smoking also restricts oxygen to the cells. If you smoke, you need to ask God to help you to stop. You need to use your faith and believe for God to deliver you from your addiction.

And another really bad thing for your body is sugar. Sugar shuts down your immune system. The whole point of raw fruits and vegetables is to build your immune system. Sugar works in direct opposition to your immune system. I just want you to choose life today, even in the foods you eat. I am not talking about a "diet" in the traditional sense. I am talking about a way of eating that gives you a better way of life instead of slowly killing you. Instead of eating sugar, switch to raw honey or Stevia. If you will change your eating to mainly fruit and vegetables, your sugar cravings will decrease and you will find it's much easier to lose weight.

Remember, this new way of eating includes juicing your

vegetables and eating your fruit. Fruit has a lot of natural sugar in it. You want two to four pieces of fruit a day. You should always avoid canned fruit because it's very high in sugar. But you need the fiber that is in the fresh fruit if you are juicing your vegetables. "But Bishop, those juicers are expensive." You will save the cost of the juicer and more on your first grocery bill when you cut some of the meat out. Not to mention the doctor bills you won't have to pay.

I know this is a lot of information but take it slowly and begin to integrate it into your life one day at a time. Everyday we all need oil in our body. But the healthiest oil comes from cold water fish such as cod, salmon, tuna, halibut & mackerel. These fish are high in omega 3 fatty acids. You can eat all of this fish that you want. It is very healthy. Chicken should be eaten only a couple times per week, but the skin should always be removed. Now when we talk about chicken and you are going to fry it, I have to remind you not to use white flour. You know that white flour and water makes paste. Can you imagine what that does in your body? If you must use flour, use wheat flour. Don't fry the chicken in animal fat and hydrogenated oils they destroy the human body. Olive oil on the other hand is healthy. Instead of using grease or vegetable oil in your cooking, make some changes by using canola oil or olive oil. You should avoid margarine at all costs, and eat limited amounts of butter. To replace butter and margarine, we use "I Can't Believe It's Not Butter" spray.   Maybe you love pancakes? I eat oat bran pancakes and they are delicious. Make it a habit to eat dark green vegetables every day—things like cabbage, broccoli, spinach, collard or mustard greens. Use olive oil instead of animal fat for flavor.

Fiber, fiber, fiber. Fiber is so important. Why? It is kind of like the gas that keeps things moving. A large majority of the cancers people get today are colon cancer. Colon cancer is very dangerous. The functions of the colon are vital to good health. To put it simply, the colon stores waste and then moves that waste out of the body. When the colon is not functioning properly, the waste remains there far too long. Fiber helps the colon to function properly. A properly functioning colon can fight off a cancer attack. How important is the colon? The colon affects your brain, heart, arms lungs, eyes and kidneys— in other words—the complete functioning of the body!

Another place that waste will try to rest is in the large intestine which can also lead to disease. If you don't have enough fiber, that stuff stays inside and that's what can cause tumors inside the intestine. You need fiber from fruits, vegetables, wheat and bran products. That is one reason that meat is so bad for you. It does not digest easily and it sits in the intestine. How do you know if you are not eating enough fiber? If you suffer from constipation, that is an immediate indicator that you are not eating enough fiber. Make sure you are drinking 6-8 glasses of water a day. Not drinking enough water can sometimes open the door to an illness. If you have trouble drinking water, try and select a special container, put in lots of ice and squeeze a little lemon in for flavor. Have it available to you all day long, and before you know it, you will have completed the days portion of water.

We all love Mexican food, but the white flour tortillas are bad for you. Switch to the corn tortillas that are fat free along with fat free refried beans. Add peppers and jalapenos if you like. Use your imagination and enjoy. Another thing is pita bread. Use wheat pita. It will be fiber in your system. For a treat, my wife and I take an avocado and smash it with lime juice, chopped onions and jalapenos. This is great on a pita. Now understand this, I am not giving you a weight loss program. This is a healthy eating program. If you are trying to lost weight, stay away from the starches, exercise and don't eat after 7:00 in the evening.

When you cook vegetable soup, instead of using meat to flavor it, use olive oil. It strengthens your immune system. There are also lots of things you can do to cut back on your fat consumption. Cut out the bacon, hot dogs, limit your eggs, use low fat milk or soy milk and let go of fried foods. Eat plenty of the dark green and leafy vegetables that protect you from cancer. In fact, tomatoes contain lycopene, which reduces the risk of colon and prostate cancer. Sweet potatoes are actually better for you than regular potatoes. But instead of using brown sugar use a sugar substitute. Start to eat brown rice and avoid white rice. And instead of eating regular pasta, try whole grain pasta or spinach pasta.

For breakfast, you should eat whole grain cereals or oatmeal. Eat all the strawberries you want. For lunch, eat salads and maybe a turkey sandwich on whole wheat bread. Always keep a lot of fresh fruit near by that you can eat as a snack. For dinner, try a salad with vegetables and some lean meat. A really good mixture is sliced cucumber, tomatoes and onions if you like. Pour olive oil and vinegar over it. It tastes awesome. Another way to season your vegetables is to squeeze lime juice on them. Try it for variety. But guess what, if you put spaghetti sauce on vegetables they taste marvelous.

"Bishop, I don't know if I can do this all the time." Let me also say that if you fall off the wagon, get back on your routine the next day. Yes, it's okay to indulge once in a while, just don't do it on a regular basis. If you go to bed on a full stomach, your body has to work all night to process the food. Exercise is very important to good health. A well-conditioned heart will beat about 60 times per minute. The unconditioned heart usually beats about 80 times per minute. The result is that the heart wears out faster. If you would exercise 4 days a week for 30 minutes per day, it would help tremendously in lowering your heart rate and promoting good health. When was the last time you got out of the house and walked briskly for 30 minutes? When was the last time you rode a bicycle for half an hour or walked on a treadmill? Exercise pumps oxygen to your cells and helps fight off disease. Exercise helps remove the toxins from your cells and eliminate them as waste. It reduces the risk of disease and helps to control weight. Check with your doctor and start right away.

People that get a lot of colds are people that don't have a strong immune system. That's why we must cut out the things that break down the immune system if you're going to be healthy and strong. You know about sugar, but alcohol will actually shut down your immune system as well. Your alcohol intake should be cut back and be very limited. We love the convenience of processed foods but they are usually high in salt and sodium. Salt has a tendency to raise blood pressure and cause heart problems. That's why you need to limit your salt intake. It is time to make a decision for health. Tell yourself "With God's help I can do this!"

This is really about obedience and determination. Deuteronomy 5:33 says, "Ye shall walk in all the ways which the

Lord your God hath commanded you, that ye may live, and that it may be well with you, and that ye may prolong your days in the land which ye shall possess."

What we are talking about here is a complete lifestyle change. Change from your way to God's way! Food is oftentimes a social event in the lives of Christians. That's okay, but make sure that the food that is included brings health and not destruction to your body. I am convinced that if you will change your diet and add exercise, your healing will come much faster.

With God's help, you can make the changes that you need to make. It will get easier and easier as the weeks go by. It may not be easy to change your eating lifestyle, but you can do all things through Christ who strengthens you (Philippians 4:13 paraphrased). Through proper nutrition and faith in God, the miracle that you need is available.

```
┌─────────────┐
│ ┌─────────┐ │
│ │         │ │
│ │    8    │ │
│ │         │ │
│ └─────────┘ │
└─────────────┘
```

NUTRITION AND WEIGHT LOSS

"And it shall come to pass, if thou shalt hearken diligently unto the voice of the Lord thy God, to observe and to do all His commandments which I command thee this day, that the Lord thy God will set thee on high above all nations of the earth: And all these blessings shall come on thee, and overtake thee, if thou shalt hearken unto the voice of the Lord thy God."
Deuteronomy 28:1-2

So far, we have learned a whole lot about eating for better nutrition and health. But many Christians face the hard battle of weight loss. In this section, I want to combine nutritional information with the keys to success in getting rid of those unwanted pounds once and for all. Deuteronomy tells us that if we will diligently obey God's Word, He will command His blessings on us. If you are eating right according to the Word of God, you will be blessed. If you are not properly taking care of your body, you are going to be cursed. That could mean sickness in your body, or it could mean being overweight and unhealthy.

People seldom die of old age anymore. Most often, illness takes them out. Things like heart attacks, strokes, diabetes, and cancer. Did you know that over one million Americans will die from heart disease this year and one-half million will die from cancer? The majority of these deaths are related to the way they eat. God says, "I have set before you life and death, the blessing or the curse" (Deuteronomy 11:26 paraphrased). "Choose today whom you will serve" (Joshua 24:15 paraphrased). Remember, God did not make you to be sick. He made you to be healthy. As you begin to grow in the Word of God, you will also prosper in your physical body. You need to make some changes in your diet so you can take care of the temple of the Holy Spirit. In order to run the race that is set before you, you must be strong physically.

Let me ask you a question. Where do you want to be one year from now? We have already learned that your body replaces every cell within one year. Are you willing to make some changes in order to walk in the blessing? If you do, you can see every cell that you have messed up by not eating right and exercising…completely turn around.

We are seeing an epidemic in diabetes and heart disease today. Many of these problems are caused by white bread, sugar, processed foods and lack of exercise. Don't forget that thirty teaspoons of sugar completely shuts down your immune system for twenty-four hours. If I get sick, I can look back and always see that I had a few days of too much sugar in my diet which lowered my immune system and I could not fight off the sickness that came against me. One soda has ten teaspoons of sugar. You might as well be drinking liquid sugar. That means that if you drink three sodas in one day, you have shut down your immune system. You have no defense against anything that comes against you.

Most processed foods have sugar added for taste. You must read the labels to make a right decision. A box of cereal may seem healthy, but if you look more closely, it is probably filled with sugar. You may as well have a candy bar. If I can get you to understand one thing that will totally revolutionize your health and strength…it would be to get the sugar out of your diet. Once you get all of the sugar out, you can start building your immune system and your body becomes the defense mechanism that it was designed to be.

Many health problems today are caused by white bread, sugar and processed foods. In your heart, you know that sugar is addictive, but did you know that it is actually classified as a drug? No matter how old you are, it is never too late to say, "Wait, I am going to get this thing turned around in my life."

Approximately one in every three adults in our country has high blood pressure. Even though half of all Americans will die from either heart disease or high blood pressure, it does not have to happen to you. Maybe it is in your family line, Grandpa had it, and your Dad had it...but you don't have to have it.

Poor diets are affecting our children in a negative way. When our children eat processed foods, white flour, sugar, etc., it affects everything they do. These bad diets cause them to make careless mistakes with their schoolwork. It keeps them from paying attention in class. I will even say that many times they get poor grades in school because their bodies are deficient in the nutrients that give them brainpower. If you look at the ingredients of the cereals that children love, you will see they are filled with sugar. The snacks that children eat are filled with sugar and have very little nutritional value. Children who eat a lot of carbohydrates and sugars are usually inattentive, spacey and hyperactive. Foods that are high in sugar and carbohydrates sedate the brain and decrease mental performance.

If you seem to be hungry all the time even though you eat,

it's probably because you are putting junk in your body and now you're craving nutrition. You are eating the wrong stuff. I am telling you that when you put good nutrition in your body, the cravings go away.

What quality of life do you want? It really boils down to choices. The nutritional decisions you are making today will affect you for years to come. Things like caffeine and sugar deplete the cells in your skin and cause premature aging. When people age prematurely, it is because there is a lack of nutrients in their system and it is showing up in their skin. If you want to look young, your diet must consist of fruits and vegetables that are full of nutrients. You will notice a distinct difference in just ninety days. Get in alignment with God's Word and I believe you can see a whole new body within one year. I am talking about using your faith in the Word of God. Read the Word, pray and take action.

Some people think that to eat healthy is too expensive. But in reality chips, sugar and fatty foods cost a whole lot more than healthy fruits and vegetables. Just think of the money you will save on doctor bills! One of the keys to weight loss is not to diet. Dieting never works because you deprive your body. Your self-will can hang in there for awhile, but then you don't care anymore. You eat whatever you want and gain even more weight. That's why you need to eat the right kinds of foods and snacks consistently. When you eat the right things, you can eat all you want and not gain weight.

An over consumption of carbohydrates and sugars stimulates your body's production of insulin, which causes your body to store fat. Some people don't eat very much, but they eat all the wrong things. It does not take a whole lot of sugar and carbohydrates for your body to store fat all day and night.

If you eat late at night, your body will labor to digest the food, which disrupts your sleep. Another thing eating late does, it causes your body to store fat rather than burn fat. Eat dinner as early in the day as you can, perhaps around 5:00 or 6:00 PM. As long as you are still up, you will burn the calories and fat.

Maybe you love potatoes? Regular potatoes are high in starch and can spike the insulin level. However, sweet potatoes are much lower in the glycemic index. But not if you cover them with marshmallows and brown sugar! I know I'm in your business now, but it is only because I love you and want the best for you. I bake sweet potatoes and spray them with "I Can't Believe It's Not Butter." I also add a little bit of light salt or sea salt and pepper. This may not be the traditional "sweet potatoes", but it is healthier and better for you.

Try to understand this, you can eat a low amount of calories but have too much of the wrong things. This explains why some people try and try and are unsuccessful at losing weight. Most heavy people constantly crave starch and sugar. The problem is that these foods keep their insulin levels high and prevent their bodies from burning fat.

If you eat a lot of carbohydrates throughout the day, then you probably struggle with your weight. That would include crackers, chips, cookies, etc. It's the high insulin levels in your body that causes you to retain the fat. A lady said to me once, "Bishop, I work out every single day and I still can't lose weight." She also told me that she was eating popcorn every night as a snack before bedtime. What she didn't understand was that the popcorn was spiking her insulin level and was causing her to retain fat.

Another interesting thing is that when you consume sugars or starches frequently, within a few hours your brain will stop thinking properly. Your hands will become shaky and you will become irritable. Your body is responding to too much of the wrong things. Not only does sugar make it difficult to lose weight, it can also create PMS and mood swings. It may even cause women to go into menopause at an early age because the insulin causes an imbalance of hormones.

One of the keys to losing weight is not to count calories, but to count your sugars and starches. Always eat foods that have a low glycemic index. Don't eat before you go to bed. Eat high fiber food and stay away from processed foods that are high on the glycemic index. Eliminate or avoid white pasta and sugar cereals. To replace the desire for pasta, try soy or whole wheat pasta. Soy is a cancer fighter and good for your body.

But before you do anything, check with your doctor. Your doctor can help you set up a healthy way of eating for life. If your body is exposed to too much insulin, diabetes can set in. If you have been obese for a long period of time, you are much more susceptible to diabetes than others. It is crucial that you obey the Word of God today and change the way you're eating and exercising.

Fiber is one of the most important items to be included in your daily diet. In the mornings, I try to eat a high fiber diet to get the day started. I use a cereal called Flax Plus. It is a flax cereal with Omega 3, and is high in fiber. I add strawberries, which are high in fiber and antioxidants. I pour vanilla soy milk on top and it is an awesome breakfast. I don't need Stevia or any type of sweetener.

9

GOD'S WAY TO GOOD HEALTH

Another great product is barley green. It is high in chlorophyll, antioxidants, fiber and it is an antitoxin. It cleans all the toxins out of your body every day. You will be clean on the inside and out. Also, oatmeal is good for lowering cholesterol, however, instant oatmeal will spike your glycemic index and cause your body to store fat. So buy natural oatmeal.

So many people suffer from chronic fatigue, and it is because of bad nutrition. If you are eating foods that spike your glycemic index, you'll feel good for a while but you'll fall into fatigue within a few hours or the reverse, you'll wake up in the middle of the night.

There are times that people feel sad or depressed for no

reason. Many times it can be attributed to improper nutrition and a lack of exercise. If you are sad or depressed for no reason, it could be directly related to the way you are taking care of your body. That's why you have to eliminate high sugar foods and avoid foods that trigger insulin in your body. Caffeine and excessive sugar have been linked to depression. Most carbonated beverages are high in both, and can rob your system of B vitamins and disturb your sleep.

The Word of God tells us that we have to cut out animal fats in our diets if we're going to live a long life. The Word tells us that we have to eat fruits, vegetables and grains. What I am saying is that in general, good food should drive your lifestyle and not bad food. If you need to lose weight, focus on eating right rather than losing weight. When you eliminate the sugars and excessive carbs you will begin to lose weight. Being overweight however, can double your risk of developing high blood pressure and heart attacks. As your weight increases, your blood pressure increases as well. I receive so many e-mails from people telling me that they are obese and miserable. I am telling you today, you don't have to be overweight and unhealthy. God has the plan that will deliver you.

"Bishop, I don't have a weight problem." Let me stress this, you can be skinny and be at risk. Good eating habits are for everybody. Make sure everything you eat contains at least some fiber. It keeps your system running smoothly. Colon cancer is killing people by the thousands across our country. It is because they did not have enough fiber in their diet to clean them out. Most health experts recommend taking a colon cleansing product at least once a year. This will totally clean out your colon and help your system function at its best.

Some people think that you have to cut out all fats before you can lose weight. The truth of the matter is that your body has to have a certain amount of fat for fuel. Omega-3 fatty acids such as, fish or flax seed oil can actually prevent depression. Something that people don't know is that you must take in fat in order to burn fat. But you want to eat the right kinds of fats such as olive oil on a salad or almond butter on dark bread rather than peanut butter. Since our brains are made up of fat, it's very important that we eat the right kinds of fat. When you eat hydrogenated fats such as margarine or shortening, the brain becomes stiff and rigid. Those excessive fats can even cause brain tumors.

How important is good health to you? Sometimes when we get older, we have varying degrees of memory loss. Memory loss can be due to drug or alcohol abuse, it can also be due to poor nutrition. But with good nutrition and exercise you can generate new brain cells. With the help of proper nutrition, you can see the symptoms of memory loss reversed.

If you suffer from migraine headaches, just know that it has nothing to do with your brain. Migraines are caused by a dilation of the blood vessels in the head. Migraines are your body's way of telling you that there is something wrong in your body. It may be telling you that you don't have enough fiber in your diet or you are not drinking enough water. Don't underestimate water. I have read statistics that say five glasses of water a day decreases the risk of breast cancer in women by seventy-nine percent. Colon cancer is reduced forty-five percent.

Whatever you do, don't forget exercise. It is so important. Even if you are eating perfectly, you must have exercise. One of the greatest anti-depressants known to man is simply exercise. Exercise decreases anxiety and depression because it releases endorphins in the brain, which elevates your mood. You need to exercise three or four times per week for at least twenty minutes per day. Use weights because weights put pressure on your bones and stops bone loss. Exercise is also very important if you want to lose weight. Exercise uses large muscle groups of the body, which raises the heart rate high enough for you to burn fat for fuel.

I don't know about you, but I love Chinese food, but most Chinese restaurants use MSG as a flavor enhancer. It's high in salt and will raise your blood pressure. When you order Chinese food, order it without MSG.

And did you know that if you drink too much caffeine or sugar such as sodas, it robs your system of calcium and magnesium? Women have to be very careful that they don't drink a lot of caffeine because it will rob their system of calcium and magnesium, which can lead to osteoporosis. Whether we are children or adults, we need a daily amount of calcium in order to build strong bones and teeth. But not everyone can use dairy products, so it is good to eat vegetables such as broccoli, cauliflower and peas which are high in calcium.

When it comes to weight loss, people talk about having a high or low metabolism. They blame their weight on their metabolism. But listen, metabolism is dependant upon muscle mass. The more muscle mass you have, the higher your metabolic rate. If your dieting does not include exercise, then your metabolism will slow down, which will cause your body to retain fat. The more muscle you have, the higher your metabolism will be.

"Oh Bishop, I hate to exercise". Remember what Paul said, "I buffet my body and make it my slave". In other words, he didn't let his body tell him what to do. He told his body what to do. Exercise can help prevent osteoporosis and arthritis. Exercise actually strengthens your bones and muscles and lubricates your joints. It slows down mineral loss and improves your overall health. There's something about exercise that will actually increase your stamina. Maybe you need to do a variety of exercises or find an exercise buddy. You can help each other to maintain an exercise schedule. If you are always tired, it's your body trying to tell you something. If you're always craving something, it's your body trying to tell you something. Exercise is often the answer.

Losing weight is really all about choices. What you eat is oftentimes more important than how much you eat. Until you are in a physical condition that allows you to do all you want to do…keep working. It will be worth it. If you obey the Word of God, you will be blessed. Make a commitment to try a better way of eating for 90 days. You will feel so much better that I'll bet that you will be encouraged to go on. God has given instructions for His people in every area of their lives. Isn't it time to look and feel good? I encourage you to make a commitment and make some changes in your life today.

10

CONCLUSION

"And God said, Behold, I have given you every herb bearing seed, which is upon the face of all the earth, and every tree, in the which is the fruit of a tree yielding seed; to you it shall be for meat."
Genesis 1:29

I know you have realized by now that God has designed a specific plan for His people that tells them how to eat. This area is so important to the body of Christ because Christians are not as healthy as they should be. I believe that if every person changed their diet to line up with the Word of God that healing lines would exist no more! We would walk in such health and nutrition that we wouldn't struggle with devastating health problems.

Take your time, read this final chapter, take notes and make sure you have the tools to start eating the way God planned for you to eat. The very first Bible diet consisted of plants and seeds (Genesis 1:29 paraphrased). Of course, they would have been whole grains with nothing bleached. Leviticus 11:9 also describes the kinds of fish that are acceptable, which are fish with fins and scales. Other types of fish such as catfish are scavengers and are not healthy for a consistent diet. Yes, I did say catfish. They may taste really good but they are not good for you. The Bible way of eating includes a steady diet of fruits, grains, vegetables and fish.

Now, I am talking to skinny people as well as overweight people. Anybody can have clogged arteries no matter what their size. Any time you see a people group that is very healthy you will usually see that their diets closely resemble the pattern set forth in God's Word. People who eat a lot of processed food are usually unhealthy. That's why you must do everything possible to eliminate processed foods and animal fats from your diet. Everyday you see people taking pills for high blood pressure, pills to thin their blood, and then they take drugs for all the other symptoms in their bodies. The problem is that drugs only treat a symptom, and they don't heal your body. The only way you can really bring healing to your body is if you have proper nutrition.

"Bishop, do you believe that there is healing in food?" I believe that God already made natural foods that will heal anything that is wrong with you. All you have to do is find out what foods bring health and nutrition. Make a study out of it. Get on the internet and learn about the foods that help the condition you are suffering with. When it comes to our diets we should think in terms of decreasing the dead food in our diets and increasing the live food. Fruits and vegetables that are raw are alive, while processed foods and cooked foods are dead. Think of your refrigerator as your medicine cabinet. Eating properly is like taking medicine for your body.

If your body is not as healthy as it should be, then you need to make some changes that will bring about healing. Be honest today and say, "Yes, Bishop, my body is not healthy, but I am ready to make some changes." Yes, of course you need to pray, but you also need to come into agreement with God's Word and make some changes. You could be killing your family and not know it. God's Word is our protector. If you will obey God's Word you will be blessed. If you disobey you will be cursed or sick. That includes your diet and the way you take care of your body, which is God's temple.

It is no accident that you are reading this book. God wants to make some changes in your life that will propel you into your Godly destiny. The Bible tells us that it's God's will that you prosper and be in health as your soul prospers (III John 2 paraphrased). That scripture tells you that God wants you to prosper but also He wants you to live a long and healthy life.

Now that you are trying to be healthy, you have probably cut back on sugar. We all love sugar, so for that sweet tooth try sugarless cookies, strawberries with low-fat yogurt or maybe nuts with raw honey. For another dessert combine sugar free jello, fat free milk and fat free cookies. It's a great dessert. Make the decision to use these types of products all the time. You will never regret it. If health is a priority for you—don't let a candy bar stand in the way. I know that I would rather be well and feeling good than sick because of a candy bar.

Occasionally, my wife and I will have pancakes or waffles. We use whole wheat pancake mix and add strawberries and butter spray. Another thing I love is peanut butter and jelly. I could eat it every single day of my life. But regular peanut butter is processed and not very good for you. If you also eat if on white bread…you might as well be eating paste. I substitute all natural cashew butter, sugarless jelly and dark grain breads to satisfy the taste for peanut butter. But don't forget that generally speaking, the darker and heavier the bread is the better for you it will be.

Make a list of all the foods that you eat that are high in fiber. Eat more of them. Be a label reader. The higher the fiber content the better. A high fiber diet eats up bad cholesterol. It also helps eliminate all the toxins and poisons in your body. Processed foods have very little fiber and nutrition in them, and can lead to a multitude of health problems. They are also high in salt and can cause high blood pressure and other health problems.

In Leviticus 3:17 (paraphrased) God tells us that we are to never eat the fat of animals. Any time families have a history of heart disease; it can usually be traced to improper diets with a high amount of animal fats. Over fifty-three percent of people in large industrialized countries die of heart disease. It's usually a result of fat deposits that build up in the arteries. That's why you must reduce your fat intake. Stay away from organ meats such as hearts, livers and gizzards. Eliminate pork, corn beef, ribs and sausage. Alright, I hear you shouting, "NOT RIBS." I am not saying you cannot occasionally eat ribs, but make sure you keep it to a minimum. Don't try to eat it every week. Sour cream is also high in fat. But you can use sour cream light or plain non-fat yogurt.

Fresh ground turkey is a great substitute for hamburger. Always remember when eating chicken, half the calories are in the skin. If we are going to live in health, we must get the saturated fats out of our diet. Use olive oil in salad dressings and "I Can't Believe It's Not Butter" for your vegetables and potatoes – it's a soy product. And don't forget that soy is a cancer fighting product. Microwave popcorn is extremely high in saturated fat. So use air-popped popcorn instead. But don't eat popcorn if you want to lose weight – it spikes your glycemic index.

Beans are extremely high in fiber and will help lower your cholesterol. So use pinto, kidney and navy beans. Stay away from refried beans because they spike your insulin levels. God knew that saturated fats from animals would be harmful to our overall health and warned against them. But there are some fats that are good for you such as olives, avocados and walnuts. Saturated animal fats are very harmful, but monosaturated or plant fats will actually lower cholesterol and enhance your body's immune system. You need a certain amount of healthy fats in your diet. The healthiest fats are found in cold-water fish, flax seed and olive oil. You should eat more cold-water fish like Salmon, Cod, Mackerel and Tuna. If you are eating can tuna, eat the albacore tuna.

The cold-water fish are what we call Omega-3 foods. They are extremely good for your heart. The number one tumor that men get today is in the prostate gland. That's why men must do everything possible to get the saturated fats out of their diets. The tumors are a result of saturated fat deposits in the body. One of the worst things in the world you can eat is margarine. Other things, which are not good for you are butter, red meat, mayonnaise, cheese, whole milk and ice cream. Mayonnaise is high in saturated fat and that's why you need to use fat free mayo and read all labels. Make sure to avoid palm and coconut oil. They build up in your arteries at a horrible rate. Become a label reader. It could save your life.

It's been discovered that certain foods will lower cholesterol that is so damaging to the heart. If you eat certain grains, beans and high fiber foods it helps lower cholesterol and blood pressure. You need to use supplements. Vitamins E, C and B Complex helps prevent fat build up in the arteries and strengthens the immune system. How do you get healthy? By building up your immune system and keeping it strong. Almonds and olive oil both contain Vitamin E, which strengthens our immune system. Olive oil also contains a substance called squalene, which fights against cancer. Anytime a recipe calls for adding oil, always use extra-virgin olive oil.

In Genesis 9:3 (paraphrased), we see that God added meat for another source of protein, but God never intended for meat to be a substitute for vegetables. The fiber in vegetables will lower cholesterol. Fruits that have seeds (apples, oranges, etc.) are loaded with fiber. Avoid canned fruit and juices. The sugar content is higher than a soda. Fiber is extremely important in preventing cancer. It binds up all the toxins and helps eliminate them from your body. Fiber even lowers the risk of breast cancer in women and prostrate cancer in men. In fact, it has been discovered that fiber is a major source in lowering blood sugar. Many people have discovered that fiber can reduce the amount of insulin they need to take. If you are on insulin today, consult your physician about adding high amounts of fiber to your diet. Diabetes is a huge problem in our country today. But, when people cut the animal fats out of their diet and eat low glycemic foods, their sugar problems begin to be corrected. Childhood diabetes is different – but can still be helped by a good diet.

Approximately seventy-eighty percent of all cancers are caused by the food we eat, the air we breathe, the water we drink, and even a lack of exercise. About one-third of all cancer deaths each year are due to the use of tobacco. Millions die every year because of cancers due to the use of tobacco. Tobacco usage is a bondage, it is a drug that has you addicted. You need God's help to get off of tobacco. Start by standing on the Word and even get counseling if you have to. You can defeat this addiction!

Cancers are run-away cells that are out of control. Tumors are pockets of toxins that your body is trying to get rid of. In most cases, tumors are fatty deposits that are out of control. Some statistics say that forty-nine percent of all Americans will develop some form of cancer in their lifetime. But only fourteen percent who exercise regularly will develop cancer. That's because exercise works the toxins out of your system. If you are always tired…there is something wrong. Check your diet. If you sleep a lot…check what you are eating.

God has designed our immune systems to get rid of harmful and abnormal cells. Cancer is a failure within the body's immune system for some reason. Do everything you can to build up your immune systems. Every morning I take barley green, which is high in antioxidants and fights cancer cells. It is also high in vitamin C and chlorophyll. Barley green cleans you out and brings great nutrition into your body. It's all about building up your immune system. I don't do this because it tastes good. I do it because it is my medicine. It's the same with the Word of God. I obey it because it is protection for me. I do it because I trust God and it will bring life to me.

These principles may sound too difficult to you. "Bishop, I sure like my fried chicken and well seasoned foods." Well, it is a choice between health and a long life or poor health and an early death. It is about being strong physically and spiritually. Take this process one step at a time if you need to. Start by drinking eight glasses of water everyday and progress from there. Next you may cut out all of the sugar in your life. Little by little you will reach your goal if you are diligent.

It has been discovered that there's a chemical in chili peppers that may neutralize cancer causing substances that may prevent cancers such as stomach cancer. This is interesting to me because when I was about 30 years old, I started having stomach problems. I would have heart burn in the middle of the night and all kinds of symptoms. My dad had stomach problems when he was thirty years old. He believed in bland food. No spicy stuff. So I grew up like this. My oldest son also had stomach problems at age thirty. One day after I got saved, God spoke to my heart. I can't explain it but after that I had the faith to eat differently. I started eating chili peppers. I did not know what I know now. Those chili peppers helped me. Now, I eat chili peppers, onions, salsa and garlic. Rarely do I have to take an antacid pill of kind.

Traditionally, Latin people use lots of peppers and spices in their food. They also have very low incidence of stomach cancer. Garlic and onions help to build up our immune system, and that helps fight cancer. If you don't like garlic, use garlic tablets. There is no odor, but you get the same benefits. God's way of protecting you from all kinds of diseases is through your immune system. It can protect you from a cold, heart disease and even fight cancer.

You should be eating three or more servings of vegetables everyday. I must tell you again to eliminate all white flour and white bread from your diet and eat dark breads that are whole grains. Your diet will determine the quality of life that you live.

Use very little salt or try light salt, or sea salt. Large amounts of salt will shut down your immune system. I have found that lemon or lime juice work very well on many foods.

You can get calcium from non-fat cottage cheese or skim milk. In fact, skim milk is a good source of vitamin D, which lowers our risk of certain cancers. Vitamin C and B-Complex help strengthen our immune systems. Beta Carotene strengthens our immune systems as well. Don't forget to juice your vegetables whenever possible. We all need to eat good sources of Vitamin C like tomatoes, fruit, broccoli, cabbage, cantaloupe, strawberries and all forms of greens. When you are cooking greens, use smoked turkey for seasoning instead of pork fat. All kinds of greens have cancer fighting properties in them. Mustard greens, collard greens, spinach and dark romaine lettuce are cancer fighters. The darker the green the better it is for you.

Tomatoes contain lycopene, which is an anti-cancer substance. Tomatoes are also high in Vitamin C, which is antioxidant. Instead of putting cheese and sauces over your vegetables, use tomato sauce. Vitamin C contains powerful antioxidants as well as Vitamin E. Lycopene that is found in tomatoes is also found in watermelon, cantaloupe, broccoli and sweet potatoes.

We all need to get plenty of antioxidants through fresh vegetables and fruits. We should eat at least three pieces of fruit everyday. Take fruit to the office and have it in your car for a snack. When your body metabolizes your food into energy it produces dangerous by-products known as free-radicals. If you burn wood in a fireplace smoke is the by-product and the body is the same way. These free-radicals will damage other cells in our body if we don't get rid of them. Antioxidants are a vitamin, mineral, or food nutrient that neutralizes them. Never peel the skins of fruits or vegetables because they contain a lot of vitamins and minerals. Now, I am not talking about banana peels, grapefruits or oranges. But other fruits just clean them and eat them.

Red wine contains a substance that inhibits cancer and helps lower cholesterol. It is high in antioxidants, which neutralizes free-radicals. It thins the blood, which helps the heart. Paul said to take a little wine for the stomach's sake (I Timothy 5:23 paraphrased). Be careful not to take this to excess. If your thinking will not allow you to drink red wine, there is red wine available that has no alcohol in it. Understand this, too much alcohol will break down your immune system.

We have access to many power foods that will help us fight cancer. For example, the Japanese have a very low rate of breast and prostate cancer. It's believed that soy products are the reason. Those products include soymilk, soy flour, soy grits, soy nuts and tofu with onions and peppers. My wife makes a breakfast using tofu. She cooks the tofu and then adds tomatoes, mushrooms, onions and salsa. It is like scrambled eggs. Another good way to take in soy is to make a soy fruit smoothie. Put one cup of vanilla flavored soy milk in a blender. Add some peaches, bananas and strawberries. It is awesome!

As you implement changes in your diet, you will see healing God's way. If you will eat lots of fruits, vegetables, grains and eliminate animal fat, you can see a better quality of life. You know that crash diets don't work. But I am telling you about a lifestyle change that will get your life in alignment with God's Word. Isn't this the year to replace every cell by eating right?

I want to encourage you to email your testimonies to me at www.dennisleonardministries.com.

Many experts say that a large percentage of health problems can be prevented or greatly helped with simple nutrition and exercise. Through modern medicine, good nutrition, God's Word and prayer, I believe that we can defeat any giant that has come against our physical bodies. Even though disease will try to come against us all, God has designed our immune systems to fight it off. That's why we must do everything possible to avoid harmful foods, eat the right kind of foods and exercise. Nothing is bigger than God and my hope is that you receive this word and use it to make a better, healthier and more prosperous life, God's way.

My Personal Notes

MY PERSONAL NOTES

MY PERSONAL NOTES

MY PERSONAL NOTES

MY PERSONAL NOTES

MY PERSONAL NOTES

MY PERSONAL NOTES

MY PERSONAL NOTES

MY PERSONAL NOTES

_____

_____

_____

_____

_____

_____

_____

_____

_____

_____

_____

_____

_____

_____

_____

_____

_____

_____

_____

_____

_____

_____

_____

_____

MY PERSONAL NOTES

MY PERSONAL NOTES